CAN YOU TELL A HARDBOILED EGG FROM A RAW ONE?

W9-AWU-716

Do you know how to cook the perfect egg? Can you prevent boiling eggs from cracking? How do you keep frozen steaks juicy?

All you need to know is here, in a treasure trove of handy hints and easy, delectable, inexpensive, filling recipes.

THE STARVING STUDENTS' COOKBOOK

THE STARVING STUDENTS COOKBOOK

by Dede Napoli

Illustrations by Rob Sterling

WARNER BOOKS

A Warner Communications Company

Warner Books Edition

Copyright © 1982 by Dede Napoli

This Warner Books edition is published by arrangement with
EZ Cookin' Book Co., 9925 Currant Avenue, Fountain Valley,
California 92708
Cover design by Barbara Buck

Warner Books, Inc., 666 Fifth Avenue, New York, NY 10103

Ⓦ A Warner Communications Company

Printed in the United States of America

First Warner printing: August 1984

10 9

Library of Congress Cataloging in Publication Data

Napoli, Dede.
    The starving students' cookbook.
    Includes index.
    1. Low budget cookery.   I. Title.
TX652.N345   1984   641.5′52   84-5207
ISBN 0-446-38145-4 (U.S.A.) (pbk.)
        0-446-38146-2 (Canada) (pbk.)

To

PAUL, with love & thanks & love
TOM & ROB, at least you won't starve
MOTHER & DAD, just for being there
HEATHER & TRACY, for all the recipes you tested
DAVID, God bless you

TABLE OF CONTENTS:

A DAILY FOOD GUIDE

MILK GROUP

Milk and cheese are good sources of calcium which is needed for bones and teeth. They also supply high-quality protein, riboflavin, vitamin A, and many other nutrients.

Amounts recommended

Some milk for everyone. Children under 9, 2 to 3 cups; children 9 to 12, 3 or more cups; teenagers, 4 or more cups; adults, 2 or more cups. Cheese and ice cream may replace part of the milk.

VEGETABLE-FRUIT GROUP

Vegetables and fruits are sources of minerals and vitamins, especially vitamin C for healthy gums and body tissue; vitamin A for growth, normal vision, and healthy skin and inner linings of the body.

Amounts recommended

4 or more servings daily, including a citrus fruit or other fruit or vegetable important for vitamin C; and a dark-green or deep-yellow vegetable for vitamin A, at least every other day.

The remaining servings may be any vegetable or fruit including potatoes. Count as 1 serving: ½ cup of vegetable or fruit or a portion as ordinarily served, such as 1 medium apple, banana, orange, or potato, or half a medium grapefruit or cantaloupe.

MEAT GROUP

This food group provides essential protein for growth and repair of body tissues—muscle, organs, blood, skin, hair. These foods also supply iron, thiamin, riboflavin, and niacin.

Amounts recommended

2 or more servings everyday. Count as 1 serving: 2 to 3 ounces (not counting bone) of lean cooked meat, poultry, or fish; 2 eggs; 1 cup cooked dry beans or lentils; 4 tablespoons peanut butter.

BREAD-CEREAL GROUP

All foods in this group furnish worthwhile amounts of food energy and protein. Whole-grain, restored, or enriched flours, breads and cereals furnish iron and several of the B vitamins— thiamin, riboflaviin, and niacin.

Amounts Recommended

4 or more servings daily of the whole-grain, enriched or restored foods in this group.

*U.S. GOVERNMENT PRINTING OFFICE: 1976—O-209-693

HANDY HINT

Know how to tell a hardboiled egg from a raw one? The hardboiled will spin like crazy.

Add a little vinegar to water when boiling eggs to prevent eggs from cracking.

BASICALLY BREAKFAST

1. **FRIED:** (1) Heat butter in skillet on medium high heat till sizzles.
   (2) Break eggs gently into skillet.
   (3) Reduce heat to medium, THEN:

   - SUNNY SIDE UP—cook just till whites are set
   - BASTED—add spoonful water to pan, cover and let steam 2 min.
   - OVER EASY—when whites are set, gently flip over with pancake turner

2. **SCRAMBLED:** (1) Break eggs into bowl, beat with fork lightly.
   (2) Heat butter in skillet on medium high heat till sizzles. Pour eggs in.
   (3) Reduce heat to medium low. Cook & stir gently till done to your liking.

3. **SOFT BOILED:** (1) In saucepan, bring enough water to cover eggs to rapid boil.
   (2) Gently add eggs (1 at a time).
   (3) Cook 3 to 5 minutes, depending on taste.

EGGS—THE WAY YOU LIKE THEM

5 MIN.

1 SERVING

BASICALLY BREAKFAST

SKILLET TOP OF STOVE

MEDIUM TO LOW HEAT

OMELET FILLINGS AND TOPPINGS

1 TO 2 MIN.

BASICALLY BREAKFAST

MISC. UTENSILS

- Scoop of HOT CHILI & handful grated CHEESE
- Handful finely chopped HAM & SWISS CHEESE
- Sliced AVOCADO, finely chopped TOMATO & BELL PEPPER
- MUSHROOMS, lightly cooked in margarine in skillet
- Spoonful SOUR CREAM & chopped PARSLEY
- Grated CHEESE, spoonful BAR-B-QUE SAUCE, & ALFALFA SPROUTS
- Crumbled BACON, sliced BANANA

BE CREATIVE WITH YOUR OWN COMBINATIONS!!

NEED: 3 EGGS
2 spoonfuls MILK
dash SALT
tablespoon MARGARINE

STEP 1: In bowl, mix together eggs, milk & salt.

STEP 2: In skillet, medium heat, melt margarine. Add egg mixture. As eggs cook on edges, gently lift edges with spatula (flat spoon), pushing to center. Rest of uncooked egg will flow underneath cooked part. *(Do not stir, or you will have scrambled eggs.)

STEP 3: When eggs are done to liking and surface is still moist, put any filling you want onto half of omelet and fold over. Cover with lid and cook 1 to 2 minutes or till eggs are golden on underside.

OMELET

10 MIN.

1 SERVING

BASICALLY BREAKFAST

SKILLET WITH LID
TOP OF STOVE

MEDIUM HEAT

FRENCH TOAST

10 MIN.

1 SERVING

**SKILLET
TOP OF STOVE**

MEDIUM HIGH HEAT

16

NEED: 4 slices BREAD (couple days old, best)
2 EGGS
2 spoonfuls of MILK
2 tablespoonfuls MARGARINE

STEP 1: Mix eggs & milk in pie pan.
STEP 2: In skillet, on medium high heat, heat margarine till hot. Dip bread slice into egg mixture, then lay onto HOT skillet.
STEP 3: Cook each side till golden.

footnote: Top with syrup, applesauce, powdered sugar or fresh fruit.

QUICK LUNCH

NEED: ENGLISH MUFFIN
MAYONNAISE
TOMATO
SLICED CHEESE (any kind will do)
BACON

STEP 1: Spread mayonnaise on halved English Muffins.

STEP 2: Top each half with slice of tomato, cheese & 1 strip of bacon (folded over to fit on muffin).

STEP 3: Place on foil. Set 5 inches under broiler flame or coil and cook till bacon is done to your liking.

footnote: Try thin slice of ham in place of bacon.

ENGLISH MUFFIN BROILS

5 MIN.

1 SERVING

QUICK LUNCH

ALUMINUM FOIL

HIGHEST HEAT (BROIL)

ENGLISH MUFFIN PIZZAS

15 MIN.

2 TO 3 SERVINGS

QUICK LUNCH

ALUMINUM FOIL

350° OVEN

NEED: 4 ENGLISH MUFFINS, cut in half
1 small can (8 oz.) TOMATO SAUCE
8 slices MOZZARELLA CHEESE
Thin slices of any of the following:
ONION, BELL PEPPER, MUSHROOMS, OLIVES,
PEPPERONI, ANCHOVIES, SALAMI

Preheat oven to 350°

STEP 1: Spread each half English Muffin with tomato sauce.
STEP 2: Add slices of any combination from above ingredients.
Ending with cheese on top.
STEP 3: Place on foil in 350° oven till hot and cheese melts.

GREEK PITA BREAD FILLING

5 MIN.

1 SERVING

SMALL BOWL

NO COOKING

Combine in small bowl, then spread in pita bread pocket:

> ½ (3 oz.) pkg. CREAM CHEESE
> 1 spoonful SOUR CREAM

NEXT, fill pocket with:

> LETTUCE, shredded
> 1 TOMATO, thinly sliced
> CHOPPED BLACK OLIVES (spoonful)
> FETA or RICCOTA CHEESE (couple spoonfuls)
> sliced BANANA

QUICK SANDWICH SPREADS

3 MIN.

1 SERVING

QUICK LUNCH

SMALL BOWL

NO COOKING

● **CARROT & PEANUT BUTTER**—Mix together:
    1 CARROT, grated
    2 spoonfuls CHUNKY PEANUT BUTTER
    small spoonful RAISINS
    1 spoonful ORANGE JUICE
        good on Wheat Bread

● **EGG & OLIVE**—Mix together:
    2 HARDCOOKED EGGS, chopped
    1 sm. (1½ oz.) can CHOPPED BLACK OLIVES
    1 sm. spoonful SWEET PICKLE RELISH
    1 large spoonful MAYONNAISE
        good on Egg Bread

● **P-NUT BUTTER, SLICED BANANAS, HONEY**
    Spread WHEAT BREAD with butter, honey, and p-nut
    butter. Lay bananas in middle.

● COTTAGE CHEESE & GREEN PEPPER—Mix together:

> ½ cup COTTAGE CHEESE
> spoonful chopped GREEN BELL PEPPER
> 1 GREEN ONION, thinly sliced
> dash SEASONED SALT

good on rye bread

● CREAM CHEESE & PINEAPPLE—Mix together:

> 3 oz. pkg. CREAM CHEESE, softened
> spoonful CRUSHED PINEAPPLE, drained well
> small spoonful SUNFLOWER SEEDS

good on raisin bread

MORE QUICK SANDWICH SPREADS

3 MIN.

2 TO 3 SERVINGS

QUICK LUNCH

SMALL BOWL

NO COOKING

HANDY HINT

Let's see: The big spoon is the Tablespoon
The little spoon is the Teaspoon

SOUPS AND SALADS

SALAD #1

NEED: ½ CUCUMBER, peeled & chopped
½ (8 oz.) container PLAIN YOGURT
dash each of GARLIC SALT, PEPPER
¼ HEAD LETTUCE, shredded

Blend all ingredients together in small bowl and serve over shredded lettuce.

SALAD #2

NEED: ½ CUCUMBER, peeled & sliced thin
½ small RED ONION
½ (8 oz.) container SOUR CREAM
quick squirt VINEGAR
dash each of GARLIC SALT, PEPPER

Mix all ingredients together in small bowl. Chilling before eating improves the flavor.

2
CUCUMBER SALADS

5 MIN.

1 TO 2 SERVINGS

SOUPS AND SALADS

SMALL BOWL

NO COOKING

3 SALAD DRESSINGS

3 MIN.

SMALL BOWL OR JAR WITH TIGHT LID

NO COOKING

● **ITALIAN**—Mix together & toss with salad:

  2 tablespoons VEGETABLE OIL
  1 tablespoon VINEGAR *or* LEMON JUICE
  1 small CLOVE GARLIC, mashed
  dash each of SALT, PEPPER
  pinch OREGANO

1 serving

● **FRUIT SALAD**—Stir together in small bowl:

  2 tablespoons MAYONNAISE or SOUR CREAM
  quick splash ORANGE JUICE (or juice from any canned
    fruit you may use)
  SUGAR, to taste
        Gently toss with fruit

1 serving

● **LEMON & OIL**—Shake together in jar with tight fitting lid:

  1/2 cup VEGETABLE OIL
  1/3 cup LEMON JUICE
  tablespoon sugar
  dash SALT
  1 teaspoon PAPRIKA
Makes enough salad dressing for several salads.

FRESH TOMATO SALAD

5 MIN.

1 TO 2 SERVINGS

SOUPS AND SALADS

SMALL BOWL

NO COOKING

NEED: 2 TOMATOES, cut in small bite size pieces
½ small RED ONION, chopped small
1 tablespoon WINE VINEGAR
3 tablespoons VEGETABLE OIL
SALT, PEPPER

STEP 1: In bowl, "gently" mix together tomatoes and onions.

STEP 2: Add vinegar & oil. Toss gently. Add salt and pepper to taste.

footnote: Try sprinkling grated cheese over or add finely chopped bell pepper.

SOMETHIN' DIFFERENT TUNA SALAD

5 MIN.

1 TO 2 SERVINGS

SOUPS AND SALADS

LARGE BOWL

NO COOKING

NEED: 1 can (6 oz.) TUNA, WELL DRAINED
1 small (4 oz.) can CHOPPED BLACK OLIVES
2 GREEN ONIONS, thinly sliced
2 HARDCOOKED EGGS, chopped
¾ cup MAYONNAISE
1 teaspoon VINEGAR
SEASONED SALT
½ can CHINESE NOODLES (optional)

MIX ALL TOGETHER IN BOWL (except Chinese noodles). WHEN READY TO EAT, TOP WITH CHINESE NOODLES

X-TRAS TO ADD
- 1 stalk CELERY, chopped
- 1 CARROT, grated
- 1 small (2 oz.) jar CHOPPED PIMENTOES
- crumbled cooked BACON
- chopped RED APPLES
- spoonful sliced ALMONDS
- spoonful SUNFLOWER SEEDS
- handful BEAN SPROUTS
- spoonful RAISINS

footnote: Filling enough for a whole meal!

NEED: 1 small bunch RAW SPINACH
½ CUCUMBER, sliced thin
1 small can MANDARIN ORANGES, drained
bottled FRENCH DRESSING (or use LEMON & OIL
   DRESSING, p. 28)
6 MUSHROOMS, washed & sliced
1 HARDCOOKED EGG, chopped

STEP 1: Wash spinach well and pat dry on paper towels. Tear spinach into bite size pieces.

STEP 2: Dump spinach, cucumber and oranges into large salad bowl.

STEP 3: Add dressing (amount according to taste) and toss gently. Top with mushrooms and chopped egg.

footnote: Toss in sunflower seeds or peanuts for great taste.

SPINACH MANDARIN SALAD

5 MIN.

1 TO 2 SERVINGS

SOUPS AND SALADS

SALAD BOWL

NO COOKING

FULL MEAL CLAM CHOWDER

20 MIN.

2 TO 3 SERVINGS

SAUCEPAN WITH LID TOP OF STOVE

MEDIUM TO LOW HEAT

32

NEED:
4 slices BACON, cut up before cooking
1 GREEN ONION, sliced thin
1 can (8 oz.) CREAM STYLE CORN
1 can CREAM MUSHROOM SOUP
1 soup can MILK
1 raw POTATO, cut into tiny cubes (½ inch)
1 can (6 oz.) MINCED CLAMS and juice

STEP 1: In saucepan, on medium heat, cook bacon till almost crisp. Add onion. Cook 1 more minute. Carefully drain grease into an old can. (Discard later when solidified)

STEP 2: In same pan, add rest of ingredients. Bring to a boil. Reduce heat to low. Cover. Cook, stirring often, till potatoes are done. (approx. 15 min.)

NEED: 1 (10 oz.) can CHICKEN BROTH
1 soup can WATER
2 spoonfuls UNCOOKED RICE (not instant)
1 EGG
small spoonful LEMON JUICE

STEP 1: On med. high heat, in saucepan, pour chicken broth, water and rice. Bring to boil. Turn heat down to lowest setting. Cook 20 min.

STEP 2: Just before serving, beat egg with lemon juice and pour into soup. Stir & serve.

footnote: When you are up all night studying, try this instead of coffee to pep you up.

LATE NIGHT CHICKEN SOUP

20 MIN.

1 SERVING

SOUPS AND SALADS

SAUCEPAN TOP OF STOVE

LOW HEAT

POTATO SOUP

18 MIN.

1 TO 2 SERVINGS

**SAUCEPAN
TOP OF STOVE**

HIGH TO LOW HEAT

NEED:
½ ONION, chopped small
1 tablespoon MARGARINE
2 medium POTATOES, peeled & chopped small
½ cup WATER
1 cup NONFAT MILK (not powdered)
SALT, PEPPER to taste

STEP 1: In saucepan, on high heat, cook onion in hot margarine till limp. Approx. 2 min.

STEP 2: Add potatoes and water. Boil gently 15 min. or till potatoes are soft. Mash potatoes with fork while still in water. Do not drain!

STEP 3: Add milk, salt and pepper. Reduce heat to low and cook till hot, stirring often.

NEED: 1 tablespoon VEGETABLE OIL
1 ZUCCHINI, chopped
1 16 oz. can WHOLE TOMATOES, cut up
handful leftover COOKED MEAT, chopped small
1 8 oz. can GREEN BEANS (or any leftover vegetables)
½ envelope DRY ONION SOUP MIX
1 can WATER (use empty tomatoes can)
small handful UNCOOKED MACARONI, (small elbow)

STEP 1: In saucepan, on medium heat, heat oil and stir in zucchini & meat. Cook 2 min.

STEP 2: Add tomatoes, green beans & water. Bring to a boil.

STEP 3: Stir in onion soup mix & macaroni. Cover & cook 10 minutes on low heat.

footnote: Very filling. Great on a cold night.

QUICK MINESTRONE SOUP

15 MIN.

1 TO 2 SERVINGS

SOUPS AND SALADS

SAUCEPAN WITH LID TOP OF STOVE

MEDIUM TO LOW HEAT

HANDY HINT

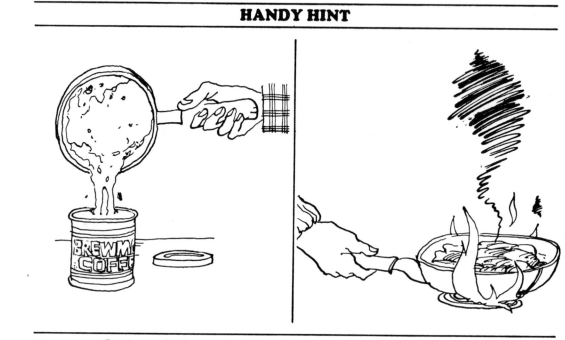

Drain cooked meat fat into old can & discard when solidified.
DON'T DUMP IT DOWN THE DRAIN!

Don't ruin fresh fish by using too high a temperature and overcooking.

MEATLESS MEALS

NEED:
1 tablespoon MARGARINE
1 tablespoon FLOUR
½ cup MILK
handful grated YELLOW CHEESE
dab MUSTARD
FRENCH BREAD, cut into bite size chunks

STEP 1: In saucepan, on medium low heat, melt margarine and stir in flour till well mixed and smooth.

STEP 2: Slowly add milk. Stir and heat till thickens. Add mustard & cheese, stirring till melted.

Dip chunks of French Bread into Cheese Sauce using forks.

footnote: Double recipe and have a party

EZ CHEEZY FONDUE

5 MIN.

1 TO 2 SERVINGS

MEATLESS MEALS

SAUCEPAN TOP OF STOVE

MEDIUM LOW HEAT

EZ TACO SALAD

10 MIN.

1 TO 2 SERVINGS

MEATLESS MEALS

**SKILLET
TOP OF STOVE**

MEDIUM LOW HEAT

NEED: 1 sm. (8 oz.) can REFRIED BEANS (or CHILI AND BEANS)
6 to 8 CHERRY TOMATOES, cut in half
¼ HEAD LETTUCE, shredded
handful grated CHEDDAR CHEESE
couple handfuls CORN CHIPS, crushed

STEP 1: Heat beans in skillet on medium low heat till very hot.
STEP 2: Turn off heat. Add the rest of the ingredients. Stir gently.
STEP 3: Sprinkle some more grated cheese on top and eat right out of the pan (saves time and dishwashing).

NEED: ½ (16 oz.) pkg. MACARONI
2 handfuls AMERICAN CHEESE, cut in cubes *OR* couple
   spoonfuls PROCESSED CHEESE SPREAD
SALT, PEPPER to taste

STEP 1: In large saucepan, cook macaroni, according to directions on package. DRAIN WELL. Remove from heat.

STEP 2: Add cheese to *hot* macaroni, stirring till melted. Season to taste. Serve.

footnote: Fast and nutritious. Tastes great with a gelatin salad.

15 MINUTE MACARONI AND CHEESE

1 TO 2 SERVINGS

MEATLESS MEALS

LARGE SAUCEPAN TOP OF STOVE

MEDIUM HEAT

GREEKS FAVORITE WHOLE MEAL SLAW

5 MIN.

1 TO 2 SERVINGS

LARGE BOWL

NO COOKING

NEED: ½ bag pre-shredded CABBAGE SLAW MIX
1 small (4 oz.) can CHOPPED BLACK OLIVES, drained
handful WALNUTS, chopped
1 small can MINCED CLAMS, well drained
couple spoonfuls RAISINS
SALT, PEPPER to taste
1 cup MAYONNAISE
1 tablespoon VINEGAR (wine vinegar is best)

STEP 1: Dump cabbage, olives, nuts, clams, & raisins into large bowl.

STEP 2: In small bowl or cup, blend mayonnaise & vinegar together. Pour over slaw mixture. Season to taste & serve.

footnote: Use as a filling for pita bread, or eat right out of the bowl.

NEED: 2 tablespoons VEGETABLE OIL
1 GREEN ONION
SALT, PEPPER to taste
splash SOY SAUCE
1 cup COOKED COLD RICE
1 EGG, lightly beaten with fork
spoonful FRESH PARSLEY, chopped (optional)

STEP 1:   In skillet, on medium high heat, heat oil till hot. Gently stir in onion, salt, pepper, soy sauce & rice.

STEP 2:   Stir & fry till rice is light brown.

STEP 3:   Add egg & parsley. Stir & fry till egg is cooked.

MEATLESS FRIED RICE

10 MIN.

1 TO 2 SERVINGS

MEATLESS MEALS

SKILLET TOP OF STOVE

MEDIUM HIGH HEAT

MEATLESS SPAGHETTI SAUCE

45 MIN.

3 TO 4 SERVINGS

MEATLESS MEALS

**SAUCEPAN WITH LID
TOP OF STOVE**

**MEDIUM TO LOWEST
HEAT**

NEED:
1 clove GARLIC, mashed
1 small ONION, finely chopped
1 tablespoon VEGETABLE OIL
1 (16 oz.) can WHOLE ITALIAN TOMATOES, cut up
1 (15½ oz.) can TOMATO SAUCE
1 (6 oz.) can TOMATO PASTE (use less for thinner sauce)
splash RED WINE
1 tablespoon ITALIAN HERB SEASONING
1 tablespoon SALT

STEP 1: In saucepan, on medium high heat, cook onion & garlic in hot oil till lightly browned.

STEP 2: Stir in rest of ingredients. When sauce comes to a boil, reduce heat to *lowest* setting. Cover tightly and cook minimum of 30 minutes (longer cooking enhances flavor).

STEP 3: Remove lid & cook 15 more minutes. Serve over hot pasta.

footnote: Freezes well.

NEED: 2 EGGS, lightly beaten with fork
1 tablespoon MARGARINE
spoonful grated CHEDDAR CHEESE
½ ONION, finely chopped
spoonful BAR-B-QUE SAUCE
large FLOUR TORTILLA

STEP 1:   In skillet, on medium heat, cook & stir eggs till *almost* done to your liking. Add cheese & onions. Gently stir & cook 1 minute. Remove to plate.

STEP 2:   Quickly heat tortilla on dry hot skillet. (Watch, don't burn.)

STEP 3:   Spread egg mixture on tortilla. Spoon bar-b-que sauce over and fold up, burrito style.

WESTERN BURRITOS

10 MIN.

1 SERVING

MEATLESS MEALS

SKILLET TOP OF STOVE

MEDIUM HEAT

ZUCCHINI N' EGGS FRITTATA

15 MIN.

1 TO 2 SERVINGS

MEATLESS MEALS

**SKILLET WITH LID
TOP OF STOVE**

**MEDIUM TO LOW
HEAT**

NEED: 2 tablespoons VEGETABLE OIL
½ small ONION, thinly sliced
1 small RED POTATO, thinly sliced
1 ZUCCHINI, thinly sliced
4 EGGS, lightly beaten with fork
splash SOY SAUCE
sprinkle PARMESAN CHEESE

STEP 1: In skillet, on high heat, cook onions & potatoes in hot oil until onion is transparent (approx. 2 min.).

STEP 2: Add zucchini, soy sauce and parmesan cheese. Reduce heat to medium low. Cook 5 min., stirring occasionally.

STEP 3: Pour eggs over vegetables. Cover and cook on low heat 5 min. Eggs will puff like an omelet.

46

USING LEFTOVERS

USING LEFTOVERS

BEEF—use in:
  Meaty Fried Rice (p. 46)
  Minestrone Soup (p. 35)
  Stir Fry (p. 103)
  Yesterdays Roast Beef (p. 57)

BREAD—use in:
  EZ Cheezy Fondue (p. 39)
  French Toast (p. 16)

CHICKEN & TURKEY—use in:
  Chicken & Potato Bake (p. 53)
  Eggs Foo Yung (p. 50)
  Meaty Fried Rice (p. 55)
  Minestrone Soup (p. 35)
  Salads, (thin sliced)
  Stir Fry (p. 102)

HAM & PORK—use in:
  EZ Cheese Sauce (p. 51)
  English Muffin Broils (p. 19)
  Ham on Buns (p. 52)
  Meaty Fried Rice (p. 55)
  Omelets (p. 15)
  Salads, (thin sliced)

MACARONI, RICE & PASTA—use in:
  Hamburger Hash (p. 67)
  Meatless Fried Rice (p. 43)
  Meaty Fried Rice (p. 55)
  Reheat Directions (p. 56)
  Reheat and *use with:*
    Cheap Roast (p. 64)
    Chicken Gizzards in Gravy (p. 84)
    EZ Cheese Sauce (p. 51)
    Meatless Spaghetti Sauce (p. 44)
    Pork Chops L'Orange (p. 71)
    Sherried Beef (p. 76)
    That's Italian Spaghetti (p. 78)

VEGETABLES—use in:
  Basic Stir Fry (p. 103)
  EZ Cheese Sauce (p. 51)
  Leftover Ham Stew (p. 54)
  Minestrone Soup (p. 35)
  Toppings (p. 111)
  See Footnote—Leftover Chicken & Potato
    Bake (p. 53)

EGGS FOO YUNG

10 MIN.

1 TO 2 SERVINGS

SKILLET & LARGE BOWL

TOP OF STOVE MEDIUM HIGH HEAT

50

NEED: 4 EGGS
dash salt & pepper
1 tablespoon VEGETABLE OIL
couple MUSHROOMS, chopped small
couple WATER CHESTNUTS, chopped small
1 stalk CELERY, chopped small
handful fresh BEAN SPROUTS
splash SOY SAUCE
handful COOKED CHICKEN, finely chopped

STEP 1: In large bowl, beat with fork eggs, salt and pepper till blended. Then add rest of ingredients (except OIL). Stir well.

STEP 2: Heat oil in skillet on medium high heat. Spoon mixture onto hot skillet. (Make about size of pancake).

STEP 3: Turn over when underside is brown. Cook till eggs are set.

footnote: Heat 1 small can Mushroom Gravy and pour over.

NEED: 1 can (10½ oz.) WHITE SAUCE (find in the soup
section of market)
handful CHEDDAR CHEESE, grated
2 HARD COOKED EGGS, chopped

STEP 1: In saucepan, on medium low heat, stir & heat white
sauce and cheese till cheese melts. Add eggs. Stir and
use.

USES: • Serve over noodles, vegetables or meat

• Toast, slice of ham, top with EZ Cheese Sauce

• Omit the eggs and use over Omelets.

EZ CHEESE SAUCE

5 MIN.

SEVERAL SERVINGS

USING LEFTOVERS

SAUCEPAN TOP OF STOVE

MEDIUM TO LOW HEAT

HAM ON BUNS

10 MIN.

1 TO 2 SERVINGS

USING LEFTOVERS

SKILLET & SMALL BOWL

TOP OF STOVE MEDIUM HEAT

NEED:
1 tablespoon MARGARINE
⅛ BELL PEPPER, chopped small
¼ ONION, chopped
3 EGGS
splash MILK
SALT & PEPPER, to taste
handful COOKED HAM, chopped small
2 KAISER ROLLS or HAMBURGER BUNS

STEP 1: In skillet, on medium heat, melt margarine. Add onion & bell pepper. Cook 3 min.

STEP 2: In small bowl, stir together eggs, milk, ham & seasonings. Beat lightly with fork.

STEP 3: Pour into skillet. Cook & stir till egg is done to your liking.

Serve over toasted Buns!

NEED: 1 medium POTATO, peeled and sliced
handful cooked CHICKEN or TURKEY, bite size pieces
½ medium ONION, sliced
½ can CREAM OF CELERY soup (or whatever cream
style soup you have)
¼ cup MILK

STEP 1: In oven baking dish arrange layers of potatoes, chicken and onions.

STEP 2: Mix together soup and milk in small bowl. Pour over top of layers.

STEP 3: Cover. Bake in 350° oven for 40 min. or till potatoes are fork tender.

footnote: Try using leftover boiled potatoes and SHORTEN baking time to 20 min.

LEFTOVER CHICKEN & POTATO BAKE

40 MIN.

1 TO 2 SERVINGS

USING LEFTOVERS

OVEN BAKING DISH

350° OVEN

LEFTOVER HAM STEW

10 MIN.

1 TO 2 SERVINGS

USING LEFTOVERS

SAUCEPAN TOP OF STOVE

MEDIUM LOW HEAT

NEED:
1 handful COOKED HAM, bite size pieces
1 can CREAM of POTATO SOUP
¼ soup can MILK
handful leftover COOKED VEGETABLES
splash WHITE WINE (optional)
couple shakes PARMESAN CHEESE

STEP 1: In saucepan, dump in all ingredients except Parmesan Cheese. Stir.

STEP 2: Heat on medium heat just till starts to boil, immediately turn down heat to lowest setting. Cook 10 minutes, stirring often to keep milk from sticking.

STEP 3: Add Parmesan Cheese, stirring till melted.

footnote: If you like it spicy, add a dash of tobasco sauce.

NEED: 2 EGGS
1 tablespoon MARGARINE

1 tablespoon VEGETABLE OIL
1 GREEN ONION, thinly sliced
1 cup COLD COOKED RICE
handful any leftover cooked MEAT, chopped small
tablespoon SOY SAUCE

STEP 1: In skillet, on medium heat, melt margarine & lightly scramble egg. Remove egg from skillet & set on plate till later.

STEP 2: In same skillet, heat oil on high heat till very hot. Add green onions & stir 1 minute. Lower heat to medium. Add rice & meat. Stir & fry till meat & rice are hot (approx. 2 minutes).

STEP 3: Add soy sauce and scrambled eggs. Stir & fry 1 more minute.

MEATY FRIED RICE

15 MIN.

1 TO 2 SERVINGS

USING LEFTOVERS

SKILLET TOP OF STOVE

HIGH TO MEDIUM HEAT

REHEATING MACARONI, RICE OR PASTA

5 MIN.

ANY NUMBER OF SERVINGS

USING LEFTOVERS

SAUCEPAN WITH LID TOP OF STOVE

MEDIUM HEAT

1. Dump leftover cooked macaroni, rice or pasta into saucepan.

2. Add couple spoonfuls water. Cover tightly. Heat on medium heat couple minutes or till hot.

3. Drain off any excess water. Then use.

NEED: 4 slices of leftover cooked ROAST BEEF
1 tablespoon MARGARINE
½ ONION, chopped
1 tablespoon FLOUR
1 cup BEEF BROTH (use INSTANT BEEF BOUILLON, dissolved in hot water)
½ cup RED WINE
couple shakes WORCESTERSHIRE SAUCE

STEP 1: In skillet, on medium heat, cook onion in margarine till golden. Quickly stir in flour. Reduce heat to low.

STEP 2: To skillet, add beef broth slowly. Stir till well mixed with flour & onion. Stir in wine & worcestershire.

STEP 3: Lay beef slices in sauce & heat thoroughly. (Approx. 5 minutes).

YESTERDAY'S ROAST BEEF

10 MIN.

1 TO 2 SERVINGS

USING LEFTOVERS

**SKILLET
TOP OF STOVE**

MEDIUM TO LOW HEAT

HANDY HINT

Don't leave perishable foods out of refrigerator. They *will spoil!*

To thaw frozen steaks, thaw in vegetable oil. Density of oil holds in juices.

MEATY MEALS

NEED: 1 lb. lean BEEF STEW MEAT
4 CARROTS, cut in chunks
2 ONIONS, cut in chunks
2 stalks CELERY, cut in chunks
1 can (15 oz.) WHOLE TOMATOES, *un*drained
¼ cup MINUTE TAPIOCA (important)
dash of THYME & OREGANO
pinch of SALT
1 heaping teaspoon INSTANT COFFEE
1 BEEF BOUILLON CUBE (or 1 teaspoon INSTANT
   BOUILLON)

Preheat oven to 250°

STEP 1:   Dump all ingredients into large oven proof pan. Cover.

STEP 2:   Cook in 250° oven, 7 hours. (Or 300° oven for 5 hours.) Stir a couple times during cooking, if you get the chance.

footnote: You'll love the aroma when you come home starving after classes all day.

ALL DAY BEEF STEW

7 HOURS

2 TO 3 SERVINGS

MEATY MEALS

OVENPROOF PAN WITH LID

250° OVEN

61

BALONEY AND KRAUT

15 MIN.

1 SERVING

SKILLET WITH LID TOP OF STOVE

MEDIUM HEAT

NEED: 1 large KNOCKWURST or BALOGNA
1 tablespoon MARGARINE
¼ RED ONION, chopped
1 small (8 oz.) can SAUERKRAUT
couple spoonfuls SOUR CREAM

STEP 1: In skillet, on medium heat, cook onion in margarine 1 minute or till onion is transparent.

STEP 2: Place meat in skillet and add sauerkraut. Cover and heat till hot.

STEP 3: Remove from heat & stir in sour cream just till hot. Serve.

BEEF MEXICANA

15 MIN.

1 TO 2 SERVINGS

NEED:
1 clove GARLIC, mashed
1 ONION, sliced thin
1 tablespoon MARGARINE
½ lb. GROUND BEEF
1 small (8 oz.) can WHOLE KERNEL CORN
1 (8 oz.) can TOMATO SAUCE
SALT, PEPPER to taste
splash HOT TACO SAUCE

STEP 1: In skillet, on medium heat, cook onion and garlic in margarine till golden.

STEP 2: Add ground beef. Stir & cook till beef loses pink color.

STEP 3: Stir in tomatoes, corn, taco sauce & seasonings. Reduce heat to lowest heat. Cover and cook 10 min.

footnote: Crunch up tortilla chips and sprinkle on top just before eating.

**SKILLET WITH LID
TOP OF STOVE**

MEDIUM HEAT

CHEAP ROAST

3 HOURS

2 TO 3 SERVINGS

HEAVY DUTY ALUMINUM FOIL
350° OVEN

NEED: "Cheap" ROUND BONE or BLADE CUT ROAST
1 pkg. dry ONION SOUP MIX
1 can CREAM OF MUSHROOM soup
ALUMINUM FOIL, wide "heavy duty"

Preheat oven to 350°

STEP 1: Tear off about 2½-3 feet of foil. Fold in half.

STEP 2: Lay roast in middle of foil. Spread both soups over roast. Wrap & seal so juices won't drip out.

STEP 3: Cook 3 hours. Be careful when you unwrap foil, so juices won't spill.

No Cleanup!

footnote: Makes its own gravy, serve with mashed potatoes & hot vegetable.

FAST AND EASY MEATBALLS

15 MIN.

15-20 MEATBALLS

NEED:
- 1 lb. GROUND BEEF
- 2/3 cup packaged BREAD STUFFING MIX
- 2 teaspoons dry instant MINCED ONIONS (in spices section of market)
- 1 EGG
- ¾ cup WATER
- 1 teaspoon SALT
- dash pepper

Preheat oven to 350°

STEP 1: Dump all ingredients in large bowl, mix well. Shape into small balls (approx. 1½″).

STEP 2: Place on a cookie sheet and bake in 350° oven for 15 minutes or till browned.

footnote: Use in spaghetti sauce, soups & with gravies. Or slice and use in sandwiches.

MEATY MEALS

COOKIE SHEET OR BROILER PAN (NO RACK)

350°

GREG'S HAWAIIAN TERIYAKI SAUCE

5 MIN.

AS MUCH AS YOU NEED

MEATY MEALS

SAUCEPAN TOP OF STOVE

MEDIUM HEAT

NEED: ½ cup SOY SAUCE
½ cup SUGAR
1 clove GARLIC
½ teaspoon GROUND GINGER (in spices section of market)

STEP 1: In saucepan, on medium heat, combine soy sauce & sugar. Stir and heat till sugar is dissolved.

STEP 2: Mash garlic clove with bottom of flat glass. Add garlic & ginger to sauce. Bring sauce to a boil. Remove from heat and let stand till just warm.

Use to marinade (soak) meat 10 minutes before cooking; or brush on meat during cooking.

footnote: Makes tough meat tender. Use on steak, chicken or hamburgers.

NEED:
1 tablespoon VEGETABLE OIL
½ lb. GROUND BEEF
1 POTATO, cut in bite size pieces
½ ONION, sliced thin
1 (10 oz.) can BEEF GRAVY
couple pinches PARSLEY (fresh, if available)
pinch of THYME (optional)
SALT, PEPPER to taste

STEP 1: In skillet, on medium heat, heat oil till hot. Add ground beef. Stir and cook till brown & crumbly. (Drain off excess fat into an old can).

STEP 2: Add remaining ingredients, stir to mix.

STEP 3: Cover and cook on lowest heat for 20 minutes, stirring occasionally.

footnote: In place of potato, use cooked noodles and reduce time in Step 3 to 10 min.

HAMBURGER HASH

25 MIN.

1 TO 2 SERVINGS

MEATY MEALS

SKILLET WITH LID
TOP OF STOVE

MEDIUM HEAT

67

HEAT N' EAT CHILIE MAC

10 MIN.

1 TO 2 SERVINGS

MEATY MEALS

SAUCEPAN TOP OF STOVE

MEDIUM HEAT

NEED: 1 small can CHILI & BEANS
1 small can MACARONI & SAUCE
handful CHEDDAR CHEESE, grated
2 GREEN ONIONS, sliced

STEP 1: In saucepan, on medium heat, dump all ingredients together. Stir and heat thoroughly, till cheese is melted and hot.

footnote: Eat right out of the pan and save the dishwashing. Good with crisp green salad.

NEED:
- 1 strip BACON, cut up
- ½ ONION, chopped
- ½ lb. GROUND BEEF
- splash SOY SAUCE
- ¼ cup WATER
- 1 small POTATO
- ½ GREEN PEPPER, sliced ⎫ or use: pre-pkg. slaw
- handful CABBAGE, shredded ⎬ or
- 1 stalk CELERY, sliced ⎭ chop suey mix
- 1 TOMATO, sliced or (15 oz.) can WHOLE TOMATOES, DRAINED

STEP 1: In skillet, on medium heat, cook bacon till done. Add onions and ground beef. Cook till meat is brown. (Drain off fat into old can, not down sink).

STEP 2: Stir in soy sauce & water. Layer vegetables on meat.

STEP 3: Cover & cook on high heat 1 min. Reduce heat to low and continue cooking 15 min.

LO-CAL SKILLET SUPPER

30 MIN.

1 TO 2 SERVINGS

MEATY MEALS

SKILLET WITH LID TOP OF STOVE
MEDIUM TO LOW HEAT

MEAT LOAF MEN LIKE

45 MIN.

2 TO 3 SERVINGS

BAKING DISH

350° OVEN

70

NEED:
1 lb. GROUND BEEF
2 slices SOFT BREAD, crumbled up
1 (4 oz.) can MUSHROOMS (stems & pieces)
¼ cup MILK
1 EGG
couple plops CATSUP
½ pkg. dry ONION SOUP MIX, (shake well before using)

Preheat oven to 350°

STEP 1: In large bowl, beat egg with fork. Add milk and bread crumbs. Stir to mix.

STEP 2: Dump in rest of the ingredients and stir to mix well.

STEP 3: Dump mixture into oven baking dish & mold into a loaf. Bake at 350° for 45 min. or till done to your liking.

footnote: Makes great cold sandwiches next day.

NEED: 3-4 PORK CHOPS
1 tablespoon MARGARINE
1 small can FROZEN ORANGE JUICE
1 spoonful BROWN SUGAR
splash WHITE WINE (or SHERRY) (or WATER)
pinch of ground ginger (optional)

STEP 1: In skillet, on medium heat, fry pork chops in margarine till light brown on each side.

STEP 2: Combine all other ingredients in a bowl. Pour over pork in skillet.

STEP 3: Cover & reduce heat to lowest setting. Cook 35-45 minutes.

Serve over rice.

footnote: Pork must be thoroughly cooked.

PORK CHOPS L'ORANGE

45 MIN.

1 TO 2 SERVINGS

MEATY MEALS

SKILLET WITH LID TOP OF STOVE

MEDIUM TO LOWEST HEAT

S'AM & EGGS

5 MIN.

1 TO 2 SERVINGS

**SKILLET
TOP OF STOVE**

MEDIUM HEAT

NEED: 1 tablespoon MARGARINE
½ small can LUNCHEON MEAT, cut in thin strips
3 EGGS, lightly beaten with fork
1 small (8 oz.) can CREAM STYLE CORN
1 GREEN ONION, thinly sliced

STEP 1: In skillet, on medium high heat, quickly brown meat in margarine.

STEP 2: Combine eggs, corn and green onions. Pour over meat.

STEP 3: Cook, stirring occasionally till eggs are soft scrambled.

footnote: Use cooked LEFTOVER HAM in place of luncheon meat.

NEED: 4-5 WEINERS, cut into bite size pieces
⅛ GREEN PEPPER, chopped
¼ ONION, chopped
1 tablespoon MARGARINE
½ can TOMATO SOUP
1 tablespoon BROWN SUGAR
dash WORCESTERSHIRE SAUCE
quick dash VINEGAR
dab MUSTARD

STEP 1: In skillet, on medium heat, cook onion in margarine till onion is transparent.

STEP 2: Dump in other ingredients, except weiners. Stir well to blend flavors.

STEP 3: Add weiners & heat on low heat 2 min. or till weiners are hot.

footnote: Good when served with Green Salad & Fruit. Also, good party appetizer.

SAUCY BAR-B-QUED FRANKS

8 MIN.

1 TO 2 SERVINGS

MEATY MEALS

SKILLET TOP OF STOVE

MEDIUM HEAT

SAUCY PORK CHOPS

35 MIN.

1 TO 2 SERVINGS

MEATY MEALS

**SKILLET WITH LID
TOP OF STOVE**

**MEDIUM TO LOWEST
HEAT**

74

NEED:
1 tablespoon OIL
4-5 WAFER THIN PORK CHOPS
1 small ONION, sliced
1 can CREAM OF CHICKEN soup
1 plop CATSUP
1 shake WORCESTERSHIRE SAUCE
splash WHITE WINE (optional)
½ soup can MILK

STEP 1: In skillet, on medium high heat, fry chops in hot oil till brown on each side. Lay onion slices over meat.

STEP 2: Stir rest of ingredients together in small bowl till smooth; Spoon over meat & onions.

STEP 3: Cover. When mixture starts to bubble, reduce heat to lowest setting and continue cooking 30 minutes.

footnote: PORK MUST BE THOROUGHLY COOKED.

NEED: 1 large fully cooked POLISH SAUSAGE
1 small (8 oz.) can SAUERKRAUT
couple spoonfuls APPLESAUCE
spoonful BROWN SUGAR

STEP 1: Place sausage in skillet

STEP 2: Add sauerkraut, applesauce & brown sugar. Stir to mix.

STEP 3: Cover & cook on medium heat till hot. (Approx. 10-15 min.)

footnote: Goes well with boiled potatoes and green salad.

SAUSAGE, KRAUT & APPLESAUCE

15 MIN.

1 TO 2 SERVINGS

MEATY MEALS

SKILLET WITH LID
TOP OF STOVE

MEDIUM HEAT

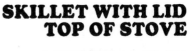

SHERRIED BEEF

2½-3 HOURS

2 TO 3 SERVINGS

MEATY MEALS

DEEP OVENPROOF PAN WITH LID
325° OVEN

NEED: 1 lb. STEWING BEEF
½ pkg. DRY ONION SOUP MIX
1 small (4 oz.) can MUSHROOMS, undrained
1 can CREAM OF MUSHROOM soup
¼ cup SHERRY WINE

Heat oven to 325°

STEP 1: In deep oven proof pan, stir together all ingredients. Cover tightly and bake at 325° for 2½-3 hours. Stir a couple times during cooking, if you can.

footnote: Serve over hot rice. Makes its own gravy. Tastes "Gourmet".

NEED: 1 can TAMALES
1 small (8 oz.) can CORN, drained
handful grated CHEDDAR CHEESE

STEP 1: Unwrap tamales & break into pieces
Lay into skillet

STEP 2: Top tamales with corn. Sprinkle cheese over.

STEP 3: Cover with lid and cook on low heat 5 minutes or till hot.

footnote: Top with sliced avocado, and spoonful cottage cheese or sour cream.

MEATY MEALS

**SKILLET WITH LID
TOP OF STOVE**

LOW HEAT

THAT'S ITALIAN SPAGHETTI SAUCE

1¼ HOURS (OR LONGER)

MEATY MEALS

SAUCEPAN WITH LID TOP OF STOVE

MEDIUM TO LOWEST HEAT

78

NEED:
- ½ lb. GROUND BEEF
- 1 small ONION, chopped
- 1 clove GARLIC, mashed
- 1 tablespoon VEGETABLE OIL
- 1 (16 oz.) can WHOLE ITALIAN TOMATOES, cut up
- 1 (15 oz.) can TOMATO SAUCE
- 1 (6 oz.) can TOMATO PASTE
- splash BURGUNDY WINE
- teaspoon SALT
- tablespoon ITALIAN HERB SEASONINGS

STEP 1: In large saucepan, on medium heat, brown garlic & onion in hot oil. Add ground beef. Stir & cook till crumbly and browned. (Drain off grease into an old can, not down drain.)

STEP 2: Stir in rest of ingredients. When mixture comes to a boil, turn heat down to lowest setting. Cover tightly.

STEP 3: Cook slowly at least 1 hour. (Longer cooking enhances flavor). Stir occasionally.

Serve on hot pasta.

NEED: 1 can (15½ oz.) GERMAN STYLE POTATOES
4 WEINERS

STEP 1: Place weiners & potatoes in skillet.

STEP 2: Cover and heat on low till weiners puff and potatoes are hot.

STEP 3: At this time to improve taste add any, or all, of the following:
- HARDOOKED EGGS, sliced
- BACON, crispy fried & crumbled
- GREEN ONION, sliced
- squirt VINEGAR, if you like it sour

Heat 1 min. Serve.

WIENERS with GERMAN POTATOES

10 MIN.

1 TO 2 SERVINGS

MEATY MEALS

**SKILLET WITH LID
TOP OF STOVE**

LOW HEAT

HANDY HINT

Rub chicken with lemon instead of washing. Flavors and cleans at the same time.

CHICKEN

NEED: 1 FRYING CHICKEN, cut up
1 small (4 oz.) can MUSHROOMS, drained
1 can CREAM of CHICKEN SOUP (or CREAM OF MUSHROOM)
½ cup SHERRY or DRY WHITE WINE
PAPRIKA

Preheat oven to 325°

STEP 1: Wash & pat dry chicken. Place in baking dish.

STEP 2: In small bowl, blend together, soup, mushrooms and wine.

STEP 3: Pour over chicken. Sprinkle with paprika. Bake at 325° for 1½ hours, or till chicken is tender.

footnote: Looks Fancy! Tastes Delicious!

CHICKEN IN WINE

1½ HOUR

3 to 4 SERVING

CHICKEN

OVEN PROOF BAKING DISH

325° OVEN

CHICKEN GIZZARDS IN GRAVY

60 MIN.

SEVERAL SERVINGS

CHICKEN

**SAUCEPAN WITH LID
TOP OF STOVE**

**MEDIUM TO LOW
HEAT**

NEED:
1 pkg. uncooked CHICKEN GIZZARDS
2 cups WATER
½ ONION, chopped
½ teaspoon INSTANT CHICKEN BOUILLON
SALT, PEPPER to taste
1/3 cup FLOUR
¼ cup WATER

STEP 1: Wash chicken & place in saucepan. Add 2 cups water, onions, bouillon, dash each salt & pepper. Bring to boil on high heat.

STEP 2: Reduce heat to very low. Cover and cook slowly 1 hour.

STEP 3: In separate cup, stir flour into water till smooth. Slowly pour into chicken & broth, stirring constantly. Turn heat up to medium. Cook & stir 2 minutes.

footnote: Serve over hot rice or noodles.

NEED: 1 FRYING CHICKEN, cut up
SALT, PEPPER to taste
1 can DIET ORANGE SODA
¼ cup SOY SAUCE

Preheat oven to 325°

STEP 1: Wash chicken, (remove skin) and dry on paper towels. Salt & pepper chicken and place in foil lined broiler pan.

STEP 2: Mix together orange soda and soy sauce. Pour over chicken.

STEP 3: Bake at 325° for 1 hour or till chicken is tender. Spoon sauce over chicken couple times while cooking.

footnote: Great to nibble on next day.

CHICKEN ON A DIET

1 HOUR

3 TO 4 SERVINGS

CHICKEN

FOIL LINED BROILER PAN

325° OVEN

CURRIED CHICKEN

50 MIN.

1 TO 2 SERVINGS

CHICKEN

FOIL LINED BROILER PAN

350° OVEN

NEED: 3-4 CHICKEN PARTS
¼ cup HONEY
2 teaspoons MUSTARD
½ teaspoon CURRY POWDER (spice section of market)
¼ cup SOY SAUCE

Preheat oven to 350°

STEP 1:   Mix together in pie tin to make sauce: honey, mustard, soy sauce, curry

STEP 2:   Dip chicken in sauce to coat well. Place on foil lined broiler pan.

STEP 3:   Bake, uncovered, 30 minutes in 350° oven. Turn chicken pieces over and bake 20-30 more minutes or till chicken is tender.

footnote: Stick a potato in oven to bake as chicken cooks.

NEED: 3-4 CHICKEN PIECES
2 tablespoons MARGARINE
SALT, PEPPER, PAPRIKA, GARLIC SALT

preheat oven to 350°

STEP 1: Wash chicken & pat dry with paper towels.

STEP 2: Melt margarine in foil lined broiler pan. Lay chicken in pan & turn to coat with margarine. Season lightly.

STEP 3: Bake uncovered 30 minutes. Turn chicken pieces over and season. Continue cooking 20 more minutes or till golden & tender.

OVEN BAKED CHICKEN

1 HOUR

1 TO 2 SERVINGS

CHICKEN

FOIL LINED BROILER PAN
350° OVEN

OVEN BAR-B-QUE CHICKEN

1 HOUR

1 TO 2 SERVINGS

CHICKEN

FOIL LINED BROILER PAN

350° OVEN

NEED:
3-4 CHICKEN PIECES
½ cup bottled BAR-B-QUE SAUCE
2 tablespoons MARGARINE, melted
large spoonful BROWN SUGAR
SALT, PEPPER

Preheat oven to 350°

STEP 1: Wash chicken & pat dry on paper towels. In small bowl, stir together bar-b-que sauce, margarine & brown sugar.

STEP 2: Lay chicken in foil lined broiler pan. Season with salt & pepper. Brush half of sauce mixture on chicken & bake uncovered 30 minutes.

STEP 3: Turn chicken pieces over and brush with rest of sauce. Cook till tender, 20 or 30 more minutes.

footnote: If too much liquid in pan, spoon some into old can.

FISH AND SHELLFISH

NEED: FISH FILLETS
1 tablespoon MARGARINE
SALT, PEPPER, PAPRIKA
2 spoonfuls MAYONNAISE
4 spoonfuls SOUR CREAM
1 small can MUSHROOMS or 6 FRESH MUSHROOMS, sliced

Preheat oven to 350°

STEP 1: Grease shallow baking dish with dab of margarine. Lay fish in dish. Dot fish with margarine & lightly season.

STEP 2: In a small bowl, mix mayonnaise & sour cream. Cover fish with mixture. Top with mushrooms (drained).

STEP 3: Bake in 350° oven 30 minutes or till fish is flaky.

footnote: Can use frozen fish, alter time accordingly, but keep oven at 350°.

BAKED FISH in SOUR CREAM

30 MIN.

1 TO 2 SERVINGS

FISH AND SHELLFISH

SHALLOW BAKING DISH

350° OVEN

91

CHEESY FISH STICKS N' BROCCOLI

20 MIN.

2 TO 3 SERVINGS

FISH AND SHELLFISH

SAUCEPAN W/LID TOP OF STOVE

FOIL LINED BROILER PAN

MEDIUM HEAT   **425° OVEN**

NEED: 1 small pkg. FROZEN FISH STICKS
1 10 oz. pkg. FROZEN CHOPPED BROCCOLI
1 can CHEDDAR CHEESE SOUP
2 tablespoons MILK
dash SEASONED SALT
LEMON

Preheat oven to 425°

STEP 1:   Lay fish in bottom of foil lined broiler pan. Bake at 425°, 10 minutes.

STEP 2:   While fish bakes—Cook broccoli according to directions on package. Drain.

STEP 3:   Gently stir into cooked broccoli, soup, milk & seasoned salt. Heat on low. Spoon over baked fish in broiler pan. Return to oven for 5 minutes.

Squeeze Lemon over & serve.

NEED: 1 FISH FILLET
½ LEMON
2 spoonfuls WHITE WINE
1 tablespoon MARGARINE
SALT, PEPPER, PAPRIKA to taste
PARSLEY, spoonful chopped

Preheat oven to 350°

STEP 1: Lay fish in shallow baking dish

STEP 2: Sprinkle fish with seasonings, lemon juice and parsley.
Pour wine over.

STEP 3: Dot fish with margarine. Bake in 350° oven, 20 minutes
or till fish is flaky.

footnote: Use sauce in pan over cooked fish.

FRESH FISH IN WHITE WINE

20 MIN.

1 TO 2 SERVINGS

FISH AND SHELLFISH

SHALLOW BAKING DISH
350° OVEN

GOOD OLE MACARONI TUNA CASSEROLE

20 MIN.

2 TO 3 SERVINGS

FISH AND SHELLFISH

OVEN PROOF PAN (OR SKILLET)

350° OVEN

NEED: 1 box MACARONI & CHEESE dinner mix
1 6 oz. can TUNA, drained
1 can CREAM of CELERY SOUP
½ cup MILK
handful grated CHEDDAR CHEESE

STEP 1: Cook macaroni, according to directions on box, using oven proof saucepan or skillet.

STEP 2: Add tuna, soup & milk to cooked macaroni and cheese. Stir well.

STEP 3: Sprinkle cheese on top & bake in 350° oven until cheese is bubbly (approx. 15 min.).

footnote: Add any leftover cooked vegetables you have to STEP 2.

HOT CLAMS N' CHEESE

10 MIN.

1 TO 2 SERVINGS

FISH AND SHELLFISH

**SAUCEPAN
TOP OF STOVE**

LOW HEAT

NEED: ½ (8 oz.) jar PROCESSED CHEESE SPREAD
2 GREEN ONIONS, finely chopped
spoonful finely chopped BELL PEPPER
dash PAPRIKA (optional)
quick squirt WORCESTERSHIRE SAUCE
1 (7 oz.) can MINCED CLAMS, *drained*

STEP 1: In saucepan, on low heat, mix all ingredients together.
Stir & heat till cheese melts.

USES:
• Fantastic as a sauce over LINGUINI
• Serve hot with chips for dip
• Dunk bite size pieces of FRENCH BREAD into
Clams N' Cheese and serve with green salad

JUST FOR THE HALIBUT

30 MIN.

1 TO 2 SERVINGS

FISH AND SHELLFISH

SHALLOW BAKING DISH

350° OVEN

NEED: 1 HALIBUT STEAK
1 LEMON
1 small TOMATO, chopped
1 CARROT, grated
1 GREEN ONION

Preheat oven to 350°

STEP 1:   Place halibut in shallow baking dish. Squeeze lemon over fish.

STEP 2:   Mix vegetables together in small bowl & spread over halibut.

STEP 3:   Cover dish with foil and bake 25-30 minutes in 350° oven.

NEED: ½ small ONION, chopped small
1 tablespoon MARGARINE
1 clove GARLIC, mashed
1 teaspoon PARSLEY, chopped small
½ lb. SHRIMP (use frozen precooked; cheaper)
½ cup WHITE WINE
SALT, PEPPER to taste
1 teaspoon CORNSTARCH, dissolved in spoonful of
water

STEP 1:   In skillet, on medium heat, cook onion in hot oil till transparent (2 min.). Stir in garlic, parsley and shrimp. Cook 3 minutes.

STEP 2:   Add wine, salt & pepper. Bring to boil. Turn heat to lowest setting. Cover & cook 3 minutes.

STEP 3:   Remove cover. Stir dissolved corn starch into shrimp & sauce. Cook 1 min. Sauce will thicken.

SHRIMP IN WINE

10 MIN.

1 TO 2 SERVINGS

FISH AND SHELLFISH

SKILLET WITH LID
TOP OF STOVE
MEDIUM TO LOWEST HEAT

97

HANDY HINT

For fresh parsley & alfalfa sprouts, try growing your own in small pots by a sunny window.

To remove onion odor from your hands, rub them with celery.

VEGETABLES

BASIC STIR FRY SAUCE

2 MIN.

1 SERVING

VEGETABLES

NEED: ½ teaspoon INSTANT CHICKEN BOUILLON
¼ cup HOT WATER
splash SOY SAUCE
1 teaspoon CORN STARCH

STEP 1: In small cup or bowl, dissolve bouillon in hot water.

STEP 2: Add rest of ingredients. Stir.

STEP 3: Pour over hot stir fried vegetables. Cook & stir 1 minute or till sauce thickens. (High heat).

footnote: If you like a "thicker" sauce, add more cornstarch

● CORN STARCH is in the Flour Section of the market and INSTANT BOUILLON is in the Soup Section of the market

SMALL BOWL

BASIC STIR FRY (MISC.)

Other Stir Fry Ideas:
Use couple handfuls of any of following:
    Leftover cooked MEAT, sliced thin
    SUNFLOWER SEEDS
    NUTS
    SHELL FISH
    CHICKEN BREASTS, uncooked & sliced thin (1/4″)
    SIRLOIN STEAK, uncooked & sliced thin (1/4″)

Use directions for Basic Stir fry (p. 103)

BASIC STIR FRY RECIPE for VEGETABLES

5 MIN.

1 TO 2 SERVINGS

VEGETABLES

**SKILLET
TOP OF STOVE**

HIGH HEAT

NEED: couple handfuls fresh or frozen VEGETABLES, cut into
bite size pieces
2 tablespoons VEGETABLE OIL
splash SOY SAUCE
spash SHERRY (optional)

STEP 1: In skillet, heat oil on high heat till very hot. Stir in
vegetables. (There will be a lot of noise and spattering.)

STEP 2: Stir quickly, approximately 5 min., on high heat till
vegetables are tender, but still bright in color.

STEP 3: Add a splash of soy sauce and sherry (if you have
some). Stir & Serve

footnote: In place of Step 3, try STIR FRY SAUCE on page 101.

BROILED POTATO SLICES

10 MIN.

1 TO 2 SERVINGS

VEGETABLES

BROILER PAN AND RACK (HIGHEST HEAT) BROIL

NEED: 1 medium POTATO, washed (leave skin on)
VEGETABLE OIL

STEP 1: Slice potato into ¼ inch slices.

STEP 2: Lay slices on broiler pan rack. Brush each slice lightly with oil.

STEP 3: Broil till brown. Turn potato slices over, brush with oil lightly and broil till brown.

footnote: MAKES A GREAT SNACK!

NEED: 1 large TOMATO (cut in half crosswise)
2 SALTINE CRACKERS, crushed
1 tablespoon MARGARINE, melted
PARMESAN CHEESE

STEP 1: Drizzle melted butter on cut side of tomato halves. Sprinkle parmesan cheese, then cracker crumbs on each half.

STEP 2: Set tomatoes on broiler pan rack. Place in broiler, about 3″ under flame or heating coil.

STEP 3: Broil 5-10 minutes or till crumbs are browned.

BROILED TOMATOES

15 MIN.

1 SERVING

BROILER PAN AND RACK
(HIGHEST HEAT) BROIL

CELERY and GREEN PEAS

7 MIN.

2 TO 3 SERVINGS

VEGETABLES

**SAUCEPAN
TOP OF STOVE**

MEDIUM HEAT

NEED:
1 stalk CELERY, chopped
1 tablespoon MARGARINE
1 (10 oz.) pkg. frozen GREEN PEAS
¼ cup WATER
LEMON

STEP 1: In saucepan, on medium heat, melt margarine. Add celery. Cook 2 min.

STEP 2: Add frozen peas & water to celery. Stir. Cover & cook 5 min. or till peas are tender.

STEP 3: Squeeze lemon on vegetables and season to taste.

NEED: 1 bunch SPINACH
¼ LEMON
1 tablespoon MARGARINE
SALT & PEPPER, to taste

STEP 1: wash spinach
EZ WAY: fill sink with water & dump loose spinach in.
Break off stems at root, holding under water.
(Spinach leaves and stems are both tasty).

STEP 2: Shake off excess water and stuff spinach into saucepan.
Add couple spoonfuls of water. Cover and cook at
medium low heat for 5-10 min. or till tender.

STEP 3: Drain spinach and squeeze lemon on. Add margarine,
salt & pepper to taste.

footnote: USE WHOLE BUNCH—It shrinks when cooked.

COOKED FRESH SPINACH

10 MIN.

1 TO 2 SERVINGS

VEGETABLES

**SAUCEPAN WITH LID
TOP OF STOVE**

MEDIUM HEAT

CREAMY SPINACH

10 MIN.

2 TO 3 SERVINGS

SAUCEPAN WITH LID TOP OF STOVE

MEDIUM HEAT

NEED: 1 pkg. FROZEN CHOPPED SPINACH
8 oz. carton COTTAGE CHEESE
tablespoon DRY ONION SOUP MIX (shake pkg. well
before using).

STEP 1: Cook spinach in ¼ cup unsalted water till tender. *Drain well.*

STEP 2: Stir in cottage cheese & dry onion soup mix. Cover and cook over low heat 1 minute or till creamy. Stir occasionally.

footnote: Tastes Fantastic!

NEED: 1 small (8 oz.) can PORK and BEANS
1 spoonful BROWN SUGAR
1 plop CATSUP
tablespoon chopped ONION
dab MUSTARD

STEP 1: Stir all ingredients together in small saucepan. Cook on medium heat till beans start to boil.

STEP 2: Reduce heat to lowest setting. Cover. Cook 10 minutes to blend flavors.

footnote: Can be cooked longer to enhance flavors.

FANCY PORK N' BEANS

10 MIN.

1 SERVING

VEGETABLES

**SAUCEPAN WITH LID
TOP OF STOVE**

**MEDIUM TO LOW
HEAT**

HOT GERMAN POTATOES

10 MIN.

1 TO 2 SERVINGS

VEGETABLES

**SKILLET WITH LID
TOP OF STOVE**

MEDIUM HIGH HEAT

NEED: 1 can (15½ oz.) GERMAN POTATO SALAD, (in canned goods section of market)
4 slices BACON
4 thin slices CHEESE, any kind will do, but "cheddar" is better

STEP 1: In skillet, on medium high heat, cook bacon till crisp. Drain bacon on paper towels.

STEP 2: Dump potatoes into skillet. Add crumbled bacon. Stir to mix. Top with cheese slices.

STEP 3: Cover & heat till hot (approx. 5 min.)

footnote: Good with fried eggs and fresh fruit. Eat for any meal.

MUSHROOMS—1 small (2 oz.) can, drained and lightly cooked in 1 tablespoon margarine

LEMON-BUTTER—squeeze ½ lemon into 1 tablespoon hot melted margarine

CHEDDER CHEESE—grated over *hot* vegetables

EZ HOLLANDAISE—cook in small saucepan, on low heat:
> 2 spoonfuls SOUR CREAM
> 2 spoonfuls MAYONNAISE
> dab MUSTARD
> 1 spoonful LEMON JUICE

TANGY SAUCE—stir together & pour over vegetables:
> 1 tablespoon hot MARGARINE
> 1 teaspoon MUSTARD
> squirt WORCHESTERSHIRE
> squirt LEMON JUICE

QUICK VEGETABLE TOPPINGS & SAUCES

2 MIN.

SINGLE SERVINGS

VEGETABLES

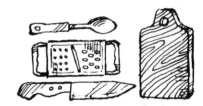

MISC. UTENSILS

STIR FRY BROCCOLI AND ALMONDS

5 MIN.

1 TO 2 SERVINGS

VEGETABLES

**SKILLET
TOP OF STOVE**

HIGH HEAT

NEED: 1 pkg. frozen CHOPPED BROCCOLI
2 GREEN ONIONS, thinly sliced
2 tablespoons MARGARINE
couple spoonfuls SLICED ALMONDS
LEMON

STEP 1: Rinse frozen broccoli in water to remove any ice. Drain on paper towels.

STEP 2: In skillet, on high heat, melt margarine. When *hot*, add broccoli, onions & almonds.

STEP 3: Stir and fry till broccoli is tender, but still bright green. Just before eating, squeeze lemon over.

NEED: 1 pkg. frozen FRENCH CUT GREEN BEANS
2 strips BACON, cut up before frying
½ teaspoon INSTANT CHICKEN BOUILLON
1 teaspoon CORN STARCH

STEP 1:   In cup, dissolve bouillon in ¼ cup boiling water. Add corn starch & stir to dissolve.

STEP 2:   In skillet, on medium heat, fry bacon till crisp. Turn heat to high and add green beans. (Be careful, it will spatter). Stir quickly 2-3 minutes.

STEP 3:   Pour broth over and continue stirring till sauce thickens. (approx. 1 min.)

footnote: Any leftover CHICKEN? Add handful thin-sliced cooked chicken during step 2.

STIR FRY FRENCH BEANS & BACON

5 MIN.

1 TO 2 SERVINGS

VEGETABLES

**SKILLET
TOP OF STOVE**

MEDIUM TO HIGH HEAT

113

TANGY GREEN BEANS

5 MIN.

1 TO 2 SERVINGS

VEGETABLES

**SAUCEPAN
TOP OF STOVE**

MEDIUM HEAT

NEED: 1 small (8 oz.) can CUT GREEN BEANS, drained
1 tablespoon MARGARINE
½ teaspoon MUSTARD
quick splash WORCESTERSHIRE SAUCE
SALT & PEPPER to taste
couple spoonfuls CORN FLAKES, crushed

STEP 1: Melt butter in saucepan. Stir in mustard and worcestershire.

STEP 2: Stir green beans into sauce. Heat on low heat till hot (1 to 2 min.)

STEP 3: Sprinkle corn flake crumbs over & serve.

footnote: Try topping with spoonful of Egg Salad

NEED: 2-3 slices BACON, cut up before cooking
½ small can TOMATOES or couple FRESH TOMATOES, cut up
½ ONION, chopped
2 ZUCCHINI, sliced in rounds
1 small (2 oz.) can MUSHROOMS, sliced PARMESAN CHEESE

STEP 1: In skillet, on medium heat, cook bacon with onions and mushrooms till bacon is done. Drain off grease (into an old can—not down the drain).

STEP 2: Add cut up tomatoes & zucchini. Cook on lowest heat approximately 10 minutes or till zucchini is tender.

STEP 3: Sprinkle with Parmesan Cheese & serve

footnote: Try adding chopped BELL PEPPERS, CARROTS, or GREEN BEANS to step 2.

ZUCCHINI AND TOMATOES

15 MIN.

1 TO 2 SERVINGS

VEGETABLES

SKILLET TOP OF STOVE

MEDIUM HEAT

HANDY HINT

If you don't have a punch bowl, use the kitchen sink—washed first, please.

When recipe calls for part of package of dry onion soup, use the rest mixed with sour cream as a dip.

DIPS, DRINKS & DESSERTS

Blend in small bowl:

> 2 spoonfuls BROWN SUGAR
> 8 oz. carton SOUR CREAM

Use as a dip for FRESH:

- WATERMELON CHUNKS
- STRAWBERRIES
- BANANA CHUNKS
- PINEAPPLE SPEARS
- APPLE WEDGES
- PEAR SLICES

FRESH FRUIT DIP

3 MIN.

SEVERAL SERVINGS

DIPS, DRINKS & DESSERTS

SMALL BOWL

NO COOKING

PARTY DIPS

3 MIN.

SEVERAL SERVINGS

DIPS, DRINKS & DESSERTS

SMALL BOWL

NO COOKING

● **DILL DIP**
NEED: 1 cup MAYONNAISE
1 (8 oz.) carton SOUR CREAM
2 GREEN ONIONS, sliced thin
1½ teaspoon DILL WEED (in spice section of market)
1½ teaspoon SEASONED SALT

Blend all together in bowl & chill. Serve with raw vegetables.

● **DEVILISH DIP**
NEED: 1 (8 oz.) carton SOUR CREAM
1 small can DEVILED HAM SPREAD
dash WORCHESTERSHIRE SAUCE

Blend together & chill

PIGS IN A BLANKET

15 MIN.

MAKES 8 SMALL ROLLS

NEED: 1 can refrigerated CRESCENT ROLLS
1 pkg. SAUSAGE LINKS (Brown & Serve type, skinless)

preheat oven to 350°

STEP 1: Cook sausages according to directions on package. Remove sausages & drain on paper towel.

STEP 2: Roll sausages into uncooked crescent rolls. (Following directions for rolling on pkg.) Place on cookie sheet or aluminum foil and bake at 350° for 10 minutes or till golden.

SKILLET & ALUMINIUM FOIL

350° OVEN

121

CHOCOLATE COFFEE

10 MIN.

ANY NUMBER SERVINGS

DIPS, DRINKS & DESSERTS

NEED: BREWED HOT COFFEE
HOT CHOCOLATE
WHIPPED TOPPING
FRESH ORANGE PEEL, grated

STEP 1: Stir together in large mugs, equal amounts hot coffeee & hot chocolate.

STEP 2: Top with whipped topping & sprinkle with some grated orange peel.

CHAMPAGNE PUNCH

5 MIN.

12 SERVINGS (1 CUP EACH)

NEED: 2 (6 oz.) cans FROZEN ORANGE JUICE
1 (6 oz.) can FROZEN LEMONADE
1½ quarts ICE WATER
2 quarts CHAMPAGNE (well chilled)
ORANGE SLICES (chilled)

STEP 1: Dilute orange juice & lemonade with ice water in punch bowl.

STEP 2: Just before serving, gently pour champagne into punch bowl.

STEP 3: Float thin orange slices in bowl. Serve.

footnote: Just before serving, try adding a pint ORANGE SHERBET to punch.

DIPS, DRINKS & DESSERTS

PUNCH BOWL

NO COOKING

LEMON AID

2 MIN.

1 SERVING

QUART JAR WITH LID

NO COOKING

124

NEED: QUART JAR with tight fitting lid
½ LEMON
CRUSHED ICE
spoonful SUGAR

STEP 1: Fill jar 2/3 full with crushed ice. Add water till almost to top of jar.

STEP 2: Squeeze lemon in. Sprinkle sugar on top.

STEP 3: Close lid tightly. Shake vigorously. Open & drink! Cool and refreshing!

NEED: 2 liters BURGUNDY or ROSE WINE (chilled)
1 quart APPLE JUICE
juice ¼ LEMON
1 cup SUGAR
1 quart GINGERALE (chilled)
ICE CUBES (1 tray)

STEP 1:   Mix all ingredients in bowl, stirring to dissolve sugar.

STEP 2:   Add ice cubes.

STEP 3:   Serve at once.

LET'S PARTY PUNCH

5 MIN.

12 SERVINGS (1 CUP EACH)

DIPS, DRINKS & DESSERTS

LARGE BOWL OR LEAK-PROOF SINK

VIENNESSE COFFEE

10 MIN.

6 SERVINGS

DIPS, DRINKS & DESSERTS

COFFEEMAKER

NEED: COFFEE
7 WHOLE CLOVES
1 STICK CINNAMON
3 large spoonfuls SUGAR
WHIPPED TOPPING

STEP 1: Before brewing six cups coffee in coffeemaker, add cloves, cinnamon and sugar to dry coffee grounds in basket.

STEP 2: Perk coffee as usual. Pour in mugs.

STEP 3: Top off each mug of coffee with a plop of whipped topping.

5 MIN.
(PLUS CHILL TIME)

1 SERVING

NEED: 2 CRISP COOKIES
WHIPPED TOPPING

STEP 1: Crumble any kind one crisp cookie into bottom of desert dish

STEP 2: Cover with layer of whipped topping.

STEP 3: Repeat. Then chill couple hours. (Flavors will blend together).

DIPS, DRINKS & DESSERTS

TALL GLASS

NO COOKING

HEALTHY CANDY

10 MIN.

MAKES 18 TO 20, 1" BALLS

BOWL

NO COOKING

NEED: ½ cup PEANUT BUTTER
½ cup HONEY
1 cup WHEAT GERM
SHREDDED COCONUT or CHOPPED NUTS

STEP 1:   In bowl, blend peanut butter, honey, wheat germ together. Roll into small balls (See footnote below).

STEP 2:   Roll balls in coconut or nuts. Refrigerate.

Eat when chilled & hardened.

footnote: To keep candy from sticking to your hands, rub a little butter on your fingers first.

Make pudding according to directions on package of INSTANT PUDDING MIX, then add to:

- BUTTERSCOTCH   — couple drops BRANDY

- CHOCOLATE   — spoonful CHOCOLATE CHIPS
  - or — spoonful MALTED MILK
  - or — spoonful PEANUT BUTTER

- LEMON   — couple drops fresh LEMON JUICE

- VANILLA   — spoonful WALNUTS; SHREDDED COCONUT

NO COOK PUDDINGS

5 MIN.

SEVERAL SERVINGS

DIPS, DRINKS & DESSERTS

DESSERT DISH

NO COOKING

PEARS IN CREAM

3 MIN.

1 SERVING

DIPS, DRINKS & DESSERTS

SMALL BOWL

NO COOKING

NEED: PEAR HALF
VANILLA ICE CREAM
CHOCOLATE TOPPING

STEP 1: Place a pear half in bottom of small bowl.
STEP 2: Top with ice cream scoop.
STEP 3: Drizzle chocolate sauce over (hot or cold).

TRY SAME RECIPLE USING VANILLA ICE CREAM &:
- PEACHES & BUTTERSCOTCH TOPPING
- HALVED BANANA & PINEAPPLE TOPPING
- HALF CANTALOUPE & spoonful BROWN SUGAR

NEED: 2 LARGE BAKING APPLES (MACKINTOSH, ROME BEAUTY)
2 small spoonfuls SUGAR
dash CINNAMON
dab MARGARINE
½ cup WATER

STEP 1: Wash apples & scoop out core (Don't go through the bottom of the apple). In center hole of each apple, pour sugar till almost full. Dab with margarine and sprinkle cinnamon on top.

STEP 2: Pour water into saucepan. Gently place apples in water. Cover.

STEP 3: Turn heat to medium and bring water just to boiling point. Lower heat & cook apples till tender. (Approx. 20 min.)

Serve with warm milk or ice cream.

QUICK BAKED APPLES

20 MIN.

1 TO 2 SERVINGS

DIPS, DRINKS & DESSERTS

**SAUCEPAN WITH LID
TOP OF STOVE**

MEDIUM HEAT

131

SIMPLE PEACH COBBLER

45 MIN.

SEVERAL SERVINGS

DIPS, DRINKS & DESSERTS

13"x9" OVEN BAKING DISH

350° OVEN

NEED: 2 (16 oz.) cans SLICED PEACHES (& JUICE)
1 pkg. YELLOW CAKE MIX
1 cube MARGARINE (or ½ cup)
1 cup CHOPPED NUTS

STEP 1: Lay peaches & juice in bottom of baking dish.
STEP 2: Sprinkle dry cake mix on top of peaches. Dot with margarine. Sprinkle nuts on top.
STEP 3: Bake 45 min. at 350° or till cobbler is golden.

footnote: Serve warm with ice cream.

NEED: 3 oz. pkg. STRAWBERRY GELATIN
2/3 cup BOILING WATER
14 ICE CUBES
1 (8 oz.) carton COTTAGE CHEESE (small curd)
1 BANANA, sliced
GRAHAM CRACKER CRUST, pre-made (in baking mix
 section of market)

STEP 1: Dissolve gelatin in boiling water in large bowl. Stir *3 minutes.* Add ice cubes and stir *2 more minutes.* (Gelatin will be thick) Remove excess ice cubes.

STEP 2: Add cottage cheese and stir well to blend.

STEP 3: Lay banana slices in bottom of pie crust. Spoon gelatin mix over bananas and chill 1 hour before cutting.

STRAWBERRY DELIGHT PIE

10 MIN.

6 SLICES

DIPS, DRINKS & DESSERTS

NO COOKING

"EZ TO FIND INDEX"

NOTES